THE FRENCH REVOLUTION

History SparkNotes

SPARKNOTES is a registered trademark of SparkNotes LLC

Spark Educational Publishing
A Division of Barnes & Noble Publishing
120 Fifth Avenue
New York, NY 10011
www.sparknotes.com

ISBN 1-4114-0431-9

Please submit all comments and questions or report errors to *www.sparknotes.com/errors*.

Printed and bound in the United States

CONTENTS

OVERVIEW   I

SUMMARY OF EVENTS   3

KEY PEOPLE & TERMS   6
   PEOPLE   6
   TERMS   8

SUMMARY & ANALYSIS   13
   FRANCE'S FINANCIAL CRISIS: 1783–1788   13
   THE ESTATES-GENERAL: 1789   16
   THE NATIONAL ASSEMBLY: 1789–1791   19
   ESCALATING VIOLENCE: 1791–1792   24
   THE REIGN OF TERROR AND
      THE THERMIDORIAN REACTION: 1792–1795   28
   THE DIRECTORY: 1795–1799   33

STUDY QUESTIONS & ESSAY TOPICS   38

REVIEW & RESOURCES   41

OVERVIEW

Historians agree unanimously that the French Revolution was a watershed event that changed Europe irrevocably, following in the footsteps of the American Revolution, which had occurred just a decade earlier. The causes of the French Revolution, though, are difficult to pin down: based on the historical evidence that exists, a fairly compelling argument could be made regarding any number of factors. Internationally speaking, a number of major wars had taken place in the forty years leading up to the Revolution, and France had participated, to some degree, in most of them. The Seven Years' War in Europe and the American Revolution across the ocean had a profound effect on the French psyche and made the Western world a volatile one. In addition to charging up the French public, this wartime environment took quite a toll on the French treasury. The costs of waging war, supporting allies, and maintaining the French army quickly depleted a French bank that was already weakened from royal extravagance. Finally, in a time of highly secularized Enlightenment, the idea that King Louis XVI had absolute power due to divine right—the idea that he had been handpicked by God—didn't hold nearly as much water as in the past few decades.

Ultimately, these various problems within late-1700s France weren't so much the immediate causes of the Revolution as they were the final catalyst. The strict French class system had long placed the clergy and nobility far above the rest of the French citizens, despite the fact that many of those citizens far exceeded nobles in wealth and reputation. Moreover, these exclusive titles—most of which had been purchased and passed down through families—essentially placed their bearers above the law and exempted them from taxes. In 1789, when France's ancient legislative body, the Estates-General, reconvened and it became apparent that the higher-ranking classes refused to forfeit their privileges in the interest of saving the country, the frustration of the French bourgeoisie reached its boiling point. The French Revolution was thus a battle to achieve equality and remove oppression—concerns far more deep-seated and universal than the immediate economic turbulence France was experiencing at the time.

It may seem on the surface that the immediate results of the French Revolution were negligible, for the next leader after the Revolution was Napoleon, who imposed a dictatorship of sorts, voiding the sovereign democracy of the Revolution. Nonetheless, the Revolution won the public a number of other victories, both tangible and intangible. No French ruler after the Revolution dared to reverse the property and rights acquisitions gained during the Revolution, so citizens who had purchased church land were allowed to keep it. The new tax system remained devoid of the influence of privilege, so that every man paid his share according to personal wealth. Moreover, the breakdown of church and feudal contracts freed people from tithes and other incurred fees. That's not to say that all was well: French industry struggled for years after the Revolution to regain a foothold in such a drastically different environment. On the whole, however, the French people had seen the impact they could have over their government, and that liberating, inspiring spirit was unlikely ever again to be suppressed.

Other European governments and rulers, however, were not too happy with the French after the Revolution. They knew that their own citizens had seen the power that the French public wielded, and as a result, those governments were never again able to feel secure in their rule after 1799. Though there had been other internal revolutions in European countries, few were as massive and convoluted as the French Revolution, which empowered citizens everywhere and resulted in a considerable leap toward the end of oppression throughout Europe.

Summary of Events

FEUDALISM AND UNFAIR TAXATION

No one factor was directly responsible for the French Revolution. Years of feudal oppression and fiscal mismanagement contributed to a French society that was ripe for revolt. Noting a downward economic spiral in the late 1700s, King **Louis XVI** brought in a number of financial advisors to review the weakened French treasury. Each advisor reached the same conclusion—that France needed a radical change in the way it taxed the public—and each advisor was, in turn, kicked out.

Finally, the king realized that this **taxation** problem really did need to be addressed, so he appointed a new controller general of finance, **Charles de Calonne**, in 1783. Calonne suggested that, among other things, France begin taxing the previously exempt **nobility**. The nobility refused, even after Calonne pleaded with them during the **Assembly of Notables** in 1787. Financial ruin thus seemed imminent.

THE ESTATES-GENERAL

In a final act of desperation, Louis XVI decided in 1789 to convene the **Estates-General**, an ancient assembly consisting of three different **estates** that each represented a portion of the French population. If the Estates-General could agree on a tax solution, it would be implemented. However, since two of the three estates—the **clergy** and the **nobility**—were tax-exempt, the attainment of any such solution was unlikely.

Moreover, the outdated rules of order for the Estates-General gave each estate a single vote, despite the fact that the **Third Estate**—consisting of the general French public—was many times larger than either of the first two. Feuds quickly broke out over this disparity and would prove to be irreconcilable. Realizing that its numbers gave it an automatic advantage, the Third Estate declared itself the sovereign **National Assembly**. Within days of the announcement, many members of the other two estates had switched allegiances over to this revolutionary new assembly.

THE BASTILLE AND THE GREAT FEAR

Shortly after the National Assembly formed, its members took the **Tennis Court Oath**, swearing that they would not relent in their efforts until a new constitution had been agreed upon. The National Assembly's revolutionary spirit galvanized France, manifesting in a number of different ways. In Paris, citizens stormed the city's largest prison, the **Bastille,** in pursuit of arms. In the countryside, peasants and farmers revolted against their feudal contracts by attacking the manors and estates of their landlords. Dubbed the **"Great Fear,"** these rural attacks continued until the early August issuing of the **August Decrees,** which freed those peasants from their oppressive contracts. Shortly thereafter, the assembly released the **Declaration of the Rights of Man and of the Citizen,** which established a proper judicial code and the autonomy of the French people.

RIFTS IN THE ASSEMBLY

Though the National Assembly did succeed in drafting a **constitution,** the relative peace of the moment was short-lived. A rift slowly grew between the radical and moderate assembly members, while the common laborers and workers began to feel overlooked. When Louis XVI was caught in a foiled escape plot, the assembly became especially divided. The moderate **Girondins** took a stance in favor of retaining the constitutional monarchy, while the radical **Jacobins** wanted the king completely out of the picture.

Outside of France, some neighboring countries feared that France's revolutionary spirit would spread beyond French land. In response, they issued the **Declaration of Pillnitz,** which insisted that the French return Louis XVI to the throne. French leaders interpreted the declaration as hostile, so the Girondin-led assembly declared war on Austria and Prussia.

THE REIGN OF TERROR

The first acts of the newly named **National Convention** were the abolition of the monarchy and the declaration of France as a **republic.** In January 1793, the convention tried and **executed** Louis XVI on the grounds of treason. Despite the creation of the **Committee of Public Safety,** the war with Austria and Prussia went poorly for France, and foreign forces pressed on into French territory. Enraged citizens overthrew the Girondin-led National Convention, and the Jacobins, led by **Maximilien Robespierre,** took control.

Backed by the newly approved **Constitution of 1793,** Robespierre and the Committee of Public Safety began conscripting French soldiers and implementing laws to stabilize the economy. For a time, it seemed that France's fortunes might be changing. But Robespierre, growing increasingly paranoid about counterrevolutionary influences, embarked upon a **Reign of Terror** in late 1793–1794, during which he had more than 15,000 people executed at the guillotine. When the French army successfully removed foreign invaders and the economy finally stabilized, however, Robespierre no longer had any justification for his extreme actions, and he himself was arrested in July 1794 and executed.

THE THERMIDORIAN REACTION AND THE DIRECTORY

The era following the ousting of Robespierre was known as the **Thermidorian Reaction**, and a period of governmental restructuring began, leading to the new **Constitution of 1795** and a significantly more conservative National Convention. To control executive responsibilities and appointments, a group known as the **Directory** was formed. Though it had no legislative abilities, the Directory's abuse of power soon came to rival that of any of the tyrannous revolutionaries France had faced.

NAPOLEON

Meanwhile, the Committee of Public Safety's war effort was realizing unimaginable success. French armies, especially those led by young general **Napoleon Bonaparte**, were making progress in nearly every direction. Napoleon's forces drove through Italy and reached as far as Egypt before facing a deflating defeat. In the face of this rout, and having received word of political upheavals in France, Napoleon returned to Paris. He arrived in time to lead a **coup** against the Directory in 1799, eventually stepping up and naming himself "first consul"—effectively, the leader of France. With Napoleon at the helm, the Revolution ended, and France entered a fifteen-year period of military rule.

Key People & Terms

People

Napoleon Bonaparte
A general in the French army and leader of the 1799 coup that overthrew the **Directory**. Napoleon's accession marked the end of the French Revolution and the beginning of Napoleonic France and Europe.

Jacques-Pierre Brissot
A member of the **Legislative Assembly** and **National Convention** who held a moderate stance and believed in the idea of a **constitutional monarchy**. Brissot's followers, initially known simply as **Brissotins**, eventually became known more generally as the **Girondins**. After unsuccessfully declaring war on Austria and Prussia, Brissot was removed from the National Convention and, like many Girondin leaders, lost his life at the guillotine during the **Reign of Terror** in 1793–1794.

Charles de Calonne
The controller general of finance appointed by King **Louis XVI** after **Jacques Necker** was forced out of office in 1781. Calonne proposed a daring plan to shift the French tax burden from the poor to wealthy nobles and businessmen, suggesting a tax on land proportional to land values and a lessened tax burden for peasants. The French nobility, however, refused to pay these taxes.

Lazare Carnot
A French soldier appointed by the **Committee of Public Safety** to help reorganize the failing war effort against Austria and Prussia. Carnot did so very effectively and made enough of a name for himself to earn a seat as one of the first members of the **Directory**. Although he was removed from this position during the overthrow of September 4, 1797, he went on to hold various posts in future governments.

Marquis de Lafayette
A liberal nobleman who led French forces assisting in the **American Revolution**. The common people of France revered Lafayette as an

idealistic man who was dedicated to liberty and the principles of the Revolution. Although Lafayette organized the **National Guard** of armed citizens to protect the Revolution from attack by the king, he balked as the Revolution became more radical.

Louis XVI

The French king from 1774 to 1792 who was deposed during the French Revolution and executed in 1793. Louis XVI inherited the debt problem left by his grandfather, **Louis XV**, and added to the crisis himself through heavy spending during France's involvement in the **American Revolution** from 1775 to 1783. Because this massive debt overwhelmed all of his financial consultants, Louis XVI was forced to give in to the demands of the **Parlement of Paris** and convene the **Estates-General**—an action that led directly to the outbreak of the Revolution. Louis XVI was deposed in 1792 and executed a year later.

Marie-Antoinette

The wife of King **Louis XVI** and, in the French commoners' eyes, the primary symbol of the French royalty's extravagance and excess. When Marie-Antoinette was executed in 1793, she was dressed in a plain dress, common to the poorest in French society.

Jacques Necker

A Swiss-born banker who served as France's director general of finance in the late 1770s, with high hopes of instituting reform. As it turned out, Necker was able only to propose small efforts at eliminating costly inefficiencies. He did produce a government budget, however, for the first time in French history.

Maximilien Robespierre

A brilliant political tactician and leader of the radical **Jacobins** in the National Assembly. As chairman of the **Committee of Public Safety**, Robespierre pursued a planned economy and vigorous mobilization for war. He grew increasingly paranoid about counterrevolutionary opposition, however, and during the **Reign of Terror** of 1793–1794 attempted to silence all enemies of the Revolution in an effort to save France from invasion. After the moderates regained power and the **Thermidorian Reaction** was under way, they had Robespierre executed on July 28, 1794.

KEY PEOPLE & TERMS

EMMANUEL-JOSEPH SIEYÈS

A liberal member of the clergy, supporter of the **Third Estate**, and author of the fiery 1789 pamphlet "What Is the Third Estate?" Sieyès was one of the primary leaders of the Third Estate's effort at political and economic reform in France.

TERMS

AUGUST DECREES

A series of decrees issued by the **National Assembly** in August 1789 that successfully suppressed the **Great Fear** by releasing all peasants from feudal contracts.

BASTILLE

A large armory and state prison in the center of Paris that a mob of sans-culottes sacked on July 14, 1789, giving the masses arms for insurrection. The storming of the Bastille had little practical consequence, but it was an enormous symbolic act against the *ancien régime*, inspired the revolutionaries, and is still celebrated today as the French holiday Bastille Day.

BOURGEOISIE

The middle and upper classes of French society who, as members of the **Third Estate**, wanted an end to the principle of privilege that governed French society in the late 1700s. The bourgeoisie represented the moderate voices during the French Revolution and were represented by delegates in both the **Estates-General** and the **National Assembly**.

CIVIL CONSTITUTION OF THE CLERGY

A document, issued by the **National Assembly** in July 1790, that broke ties with the Catholic Church and established a national church system in France with a process for the election of regional bishops. The document angered the pope and church officials and turned many French Catholics against the revolutionaries.

COMMITTEE OF PUBLIC SAFETY

A body, chaired by **Maximilien Robespierre**, to which the **National Convention** gave dictatorial powers in April 1793 in an attempt to deal with France's wars abroad and economic problems at home. Although the committee led off its tenure with an impressive war effort and economy-salvaging initiatives, things took a turn for the worse when Robespierre began his violent **Reign of Terror** in late 1793.

CONSTITUTION OF 1791

The new French constitution that in 1791 established a **constitutional monarchy**, or limited monarchy, with all executive power answerable to a legislative assembly. Under the new constitution, King **Louis XVI** could only temporarily veto legislation passed by the assembly. The constitution restricted voting in the assembly to the upper and middle classes of French society and abolished "nobility" as a legal order.

DECLARATION OF PILLNITZ

An August 27, 1791, warning from **Prussia** and **Austria** announcing that they would intervene militarily in France if any harm came to King **Louis XVI**, who had just been captured trying to escape with his family from Paris. The declaration prompted then–Legislative Assembly leader **Jacques-Pierre Brissot** to declare war on Austria and Prussia.

DECLARATION OF THE RIGHTS OF MAN AND OF THE CITIZEN

A document, issued by the **National Assembly** on August 26, 1789, that granted sovereignty to all French people. The declaration, which drew from the ideas of some of the **Enlightenment**'s greatest thinkers, asserted that liberty is a "natural" and "imprescriptible" right of man and that "men are born and remain free and equal in rights."

DIRECTORY

The new executive branch established by the constitution written during the moderate **Thermidorian Reaction** of 1794–1795. The Directory was appointed by the legislative assembly. However, after 1797 election results proved unfavorable to elements in the Directory, it orchestrated an overthrow of the assembly and maintained dubious control over France until it was overthrown by **Napoleon Bonaparte** in 1799.

ESTATES-GENERAL

A medieval representative institution in France that had not met for 175 years before King **Louis XVI** reconvened it on May 5, 1789, to deal with the looming financial crisis. Consisting of three **estates**—the **clergy**, **nobility**, and **commoners**, respectively—the Estates-General was the only group that would be able to force the assorted

French **parlements** into accepting the controller general of finance **Charles de Calonne**'s tax decrees.

GIRONDINS
The name given to the moderates in the **National Convention**. The Girondins controlled the legislative assembly until 1793, when, with the war going poorly and food shortages hurting French peasants, the **Jacobins** ousted them from power.

GREAT FEAR
A period in July and August 1789 during which rural peasants revolted against their feudal landlords and wreaked havoc in the French countryside.

JACOBINS
The radical wing of representatives in the **National Convention**, named for their secret meeting place in the Jacobin Club, in an abandoned Paris monastery. Led by **Maximilien Robespierre**, the Jacobins called for democratic solutions to France's problems and spoke for the urban poor and French peasantry. The Jacobins took control of the convention, and France itself, from 1793 to 1794. As Robespierre became increasingly concerned with counterrevolutionary threats, he instituted a brutal period of public executions known as the **Reign of Terror**.

LIMITED MONARCHY
Also known as **constitutional monarchy**, a system of government in which a king or queen reigns as head of state but with power that is limited by real power lying in a **legislature** and an independent **court system**.

MONARCHY
The form of government, common to most European countries at the time of the French Revolution, in which one king or queen, from a designated royal **dynasty**, holds control over policy and has the final say on all such matters. In France, the Bourbon family held the monarchy, with **Louis XVI** as king at the time of the Revolution.

NATIONAL ASSEMBLY
The name given to the **Third Estate** after it separated from the **Estates-General** in 1789. As a body, the National Assembly claimed to legitimately represent the French population. The assembly dissolved in 1791 so that new elections could take place under the new constitution.

NATIONAL CONVENTION

The body that replaced the **Legislative Assembly** following a successful election in 1792. As one of its first actions, the convention declared the French monarchy abolished on September 21, 1792, and on the following day declared France a **republic**. Though originally dominated by moderates, the convention became controlled by radical **Jacobins** in 1793.

PARLEMENTS

A set of thirteen provincial judicial boards—one based in Paris and the other twelve in major provincial cities—that constituted the independent **judiciary** of France. The parlements held the power of recording royal decrees, meaning that if a parlement refused to record an edict, the edict would never be implemented in that district.

REIGN OF TERROR

A ten-month period of oppression and execution from late 1793 to mid-1794, organized by **Maximilien Robespierre** and the **Committee of Public Safety** to suppress any potential enemies of the radical Revolution. The Reign of Terror ended with the fall of Robespierre, who was arrested and executed in July 1794. Robespierre's execution ushered in the **Thermidorian Reaction** of 1794–1795 and the establishment of the **Directory** as the head of France's executive government.

SANS-CULOTTES

Urban workers and peasants, whose name—literally, "without culottes," the knee-breeches that the privileged wore—signified their wish to distinguish themselves from the high classes. The mob mentality of the sans-culottes constituted the most radical element of the Revolution.

TENNIS COURT OATH

A June 20, 1789, oath sworn by members of the **Third Estate** who had just formed the **National Assembly** and were locked out of the meeting of the **Estates-General**. Meeting at a nearby tennis court, these members of the Third Estate pledged to remain together until they had drafted and passed a new constitution.

THERMIDORIAN REACTION

The post–**Reign of Terror** period ushered in by the execution of **Maximilien Robespierre** in July 1794 and the reassertion of moderate power over the French Revolution. The Thermidorian Reaction brought the Revolution's focus back to the first stage of moderate changes designed to benefit the business classes of French society.

THIRD ESTATE

One of the three **estates** in the **Estates-General**, consisting of the commoners of France, whether rich merchants or poor peasants. Despite the fact that it constituted the vast majority of the French population, the Third Estate had just one vote in the Estates-General—the same vote that the much smaller First Estate (clergy) and Second Estate (nobility) each had. Frustrated with its political impotence, the Third Estate broke from the Estates-General on June 17, 1789, and declared itself the **National Assembly**.

TUILERIES

The palace in Paris in which King **Louis XVI** and his family were placed under house arrest after they were forcibly taken from their court at **Versailles**. The point of removing the royal family to Paris was to allow the people to keep a close watch on their actions.

VERSAILLES

The royal palace built by King **Louis XIV** a few miles outside of Paris. Known for its extraordinary splendor, extravagance, and immense size, Versailles was the home of the king, queen, and all members of the royal family, along with high government officials and select nobles. On October 5, 1789, a mob of angry and hungry French women marched on Versailles, bringing the royal family back to Paris to deal with the food shortage.

Summary & Analysis

France's Financial Crisis: 1783–1788

Event Outline

1756–1783	France builds up enormous debt by participating in the Seven Years' War and American Revolution
November 2, 1783	Louis XVI appoints Charles de Calonne controller general of finance
February 22, 1787	Assembly of Notables convenes, rejects Calonne's debt-relief proposals

Key People

Louis XVI	French king of the Bourbon dynasty who took the throne in 1774; inherited massive debt problems but was unable to fix them
Marie-Antoinette	Wife of Louis XVI, whose self-indulgent tendencies became a symbol of royal excess and extravagance
Charles de Calonne	Controller general of finances appointed by Louis XVI in 1783; recommended across-the-board taxation as the only way to salvage France's dire financial situation

The French Monarchy and Parlements

The French royalty in the years prior to the French Revolution were a study in corruption and excess. France had long subscribed to the idea of **divine right**, which maintained that kings were selected by God and thus perpetually entitled to the throne. This doctrine resulted in a system of **absolute rule** and provided the commoners with absolutely no input into the governance of their country.

In addition, there was no universal law in France at the time. Rather, laws varied by region and were enforced by the local **parlements** (provincial judicial boards), guilds, or religious groups. Moreover, each of those sovereign courts had to approve any royal decrees by the king if these decrees were to come into effect. As a result, the king was virtually powerless to do anything that would have a negative effect on any regional government. Ironically, this "checks and balances" system operated in a government rife with corruption and operating without the support of the majority.

Power Abuses and Unfair Taxation

The monarchs of the **Bourbon dynasty**, the French nobility, and the clergy became increasingly egregious in their abuses of power in the late 1700s. They bound the French peasantry into compromising **feudal** obligations and refused to contribute any **tax revenue** to the

French government. This blatantly unfair taxation arrangement did little to endear the aristocracy to the common people.

FRANCE'S DEBT PROBLEMS

A number of ill-advised financial maneuvers in the late 1700s worsened the financial situation of the already cash-strapped French government. France's prolonged involvement in the **Seven Years' War** of 1756–1763 drained the treasury, as did the country's participation in the **American Revolution** of 1775–1783. Aggravating the situation was the fact that the government had a sizable army and navy to maintain, which was an expenditure of particular importance during those volatile times. Moreover, in the typical indulgent fashion that so irked the common folk, mammoth costs associated with the upkeep of King **Louis XVI**'s extravagant palace at **Versailles** and the frivolous spending of the queen, **Marie-Antoinette**, did little to relieve the growing debt. These decades of fiscal irresponsibility were one of the primary factors that led to the French Revolution. France had long been recognized as a prosperous country, and were it not for its involvement in costly wars and its aristocracy's extravagant spending, it might have remained one.

CHARLES DE CALONNE

Finally, in the early 1780s, France realized that it had to address the problem, and fast. First, Louis XVI appointed **Charles de Calonne** controller general of finances in 1783. Then, in 1786, the French government, worried about unrest should it to try to raise taxes on the peasants, yet reluctant to ask the nobles for money, approached various European banks in search of a loan. By that point, however, most of Europe knew the depth of France's financial woes, so the country found itself with no credibility.

Louis XVI asked Calonne to evaluate the situation and propose a solution. Charged with auditing all of the royal accounts and records, Calonne found a financial system in shambles. Independent accountants had been put in charge of various tasks regarding the acquisition and distribution of government funds, which made the tracking of such transactions very difficult. Furthermore, the arrangement had left the door wide open to corruption, enabling many of the accountants to dip into government funds for their own use. As for raising new money, the only system in place was **taxation**. At the time, however, taxation only applied to peasants. The nobility were tax-exempt, and the parlements would never agree to across-the-board tax increases.

THE ASSEMBLY OF NOTABLES

Calonne finally convinced Louis XVI to gather the nobility together for a conference, during which Calonne and the king could fully explain the tenuous situation facing France. This gathering, dubbed the **Assembly of Notables**, turned out to be a virtual who's who of people who didn't want to pay any taxes. After giving his presentation, Calonne urged the notables either to agree to the new taxes or to forfeit their exemption to the current ones. Unsurprisingly, the notables refused both plans and turned against Calonne, questioning the validity of his work. He was dismissed shortly thereafter, leaving France's economic prospects even grimmer than before.

REVOLUTION ON THE HORIZON

By the late 1780s, it was becoming increasingly clear that the system in place under the Old Regime in France simply could not last. It was too irresponsible and oppressed too many people. Furthermore, as the result of the **Enlightenment**, secularism was spreading in France, religious thought was becoming divided, and the religious justifications for rule—divine right and absolutism—were losing credibility. The aristocracy and royalty, however, ignored these progressive trends in French thought and society. Rather, the royals and nobles adhered even more firmly to tradition and archaic law. As it would turn out, their intractability would cost them everything that they were trying to preserve.

THE BOURGEOISIE

Although many accounts of the French Revolution focus on the French peasantry's grievances—rising food prices, disadvantageous feudal contracts, and general mistreatment at the hands of the aristocracy—these factors actually played a limited role in inciting the Revolution. For all of the hardships that they endured, it wasn't the peasants who jump-started the Revolution. Rather, it was the wealthy commoners—the **bourgeoisie**—who objected most vocally to the subpar treatment they were receiving. The bourgeoisie were generally hardworking, educated men who were well versed in the enlightened thought of the time. Although many of the wealthier members of the bourgeoisie had more money than some of the French nobles, they lacked elite titles and thus were subjected to the same treatment and taxation as even the poorest peasants. It was the bourgeoisie that would really act as a catalyst for the Revolution, and once they started to act, the peasants were soon to follow.

THE ESTATES-GENERAL: 1789

EVENTS

May 5, 1789	Louis XVI summons Estates-General for its first meeting since 1614
June 17	Third Estate breaks away from Estates-General, establishes itself as National Assembly

KEY PEOPLE

Jacques Necker	Director general of finance who returned to office after Calonne's dismissal
Emmanuel-Joseph Sieyès	Author of influential "What Is the Third Estate?" pamphlet, which influenced the Third Estate to break off from the Estates-General

NECKER AND THE ESTATES-GENERAL

In the wake of Calonne's dismissal, Louis XVI brought back Swiss banker **Jacques Necker**, who had previously served a ten-year stint as director general of finance. After assessing the situation, Necker insisted that Louis XVI call together the **Estates-General**, a French congress that originated in the medieval period and consisted of three **estates**. The **First Estate** was the clergy, the **Second Estate** the nobility, and the **Third Estate** effectively the rest of French society.

On May 5, 1789, Louis XVI convened the Estates-General. Almost immediately, it became apparent that this archaic arrangement—the group had last been assembled in 1614—would not sit well with its present members. Although Louis XVI granted the Third Estate greater numerical representation, the **Parlement of Paris** stepped in and invoked an old rule mandating that each estate receive one vote, regardless of size. As a result, though the Third Estate was vastly larger than the clergy and nobility, each estate had the same representation—one vote. Inevitably, the Third Estate's vote was overridden by the combined votes of the clergy and nobility.

RESENTMENT AGAINST THE CHURCH

The fact that the Estates-General hadn't been summoned in nearly 200 years probably says a thing or two about its effectiveness. The First and Second Estates—clergy and nobility, respectively—were too closely related in many matters. Both were linked intrinsically to the royalty and shared many similar privileges. As a result, their votes often went the same way, automatically neutralizing any effort by the Third Estate.

Additionally, in a country as secularized as France at the time, giving the church a full third of the vote was ill-advised: although

France's citizens would ultimately have their revenge, at the time the church's voting power just fostered more animosity. There were numerous philosophers in France speaking out against religion and the mindless following that it supposedly demanded, and many resented being forced to follow the decisions of the church on a national scale.

DIVIDES IN THE THIRD ESTATE

Beyond the chasm that existed between it and the other estates, the Third Estate itself varied greatly in socioeconomic status: some members were peasants and laborers, whereas others had the occupations, wealth, and lifestyles of nobility. These disparities between members of the Third Estate made it difficult for the wealthy members to relate to the peasants with whom they were grouped. Because of these rifts, the Estates-General, though organized to reach a peaceful solution, remained in a prolonged internal feud. It was only through the efforts of men such as Emmanuel-Joseph Sieyès (*see below*) that the members of the Third Estate finally realized that fighting among themselves was fruitless and that if they took advantage of the estate's massive size, they would be a force that could not be ignored.

"WHAT IS THE THIRD ESTATE?"

To add insult to injury, delegates from the Third Estate were forced to wear traditional black robes and to enter the Estates-General meeting hall by a side door. Necker tried to placate the Third Estate into tolerating these slights until some progress could be made, but his diplomatic efforts accomplished little. Fed up with their mistreatment, activists and pamphleteers of the Third Estate took to the streets in protest.

The most famous effort was a pamphlet written by liberal clergy member **Emmanuel-Joseph Sieyès** titled **"What Is the Third Estate?"** In response to his own question, Sieyès answered, "The Nation." The pamphlet articulated the pervasive feeling in France that though a small minority might be in control, the country truly belonged to the masses. Sieyès's pamphlet compelled the Third Estate to action, inciting the masses to take matters into their own hands if the aristocracy failed to give them due respect.

THE THIRD ESTATE'S REVOLT

As the impasse in the Estates-General continued, the Third Estate became more convinced of its entitlement to liberty. Seeing that neither the king nor the other estates would acquiesce to its requests, the Third Estate began to organize within itself and recruit actively from the other estates. On June 17, 1789, bolstered by community-wide support, the Third Estate officially broke away from the Estates-General and proclaimed itself the **National Assembly**. In so doing, it also granted itself control over taxation. Shortly thereafter, many members of the other estates joined the cause.

BLAMING THE ARISTOCRACY

Although the reconvening of the Estates-General presented France's aristocracy and clergy with a perfect opportunity to appease the Third Estate and maintain control, they focused only on maintaining the dominance of their respective estates rather than address the important issues that plagued the country. When the Estates-General convened, the Third Estate wasn't seeking a revolution—just a bit of liberty and a more equitable tax burden. The entire Revolution might have been avoided had the first two estates simply acquiesced to some of the Third Estate's moderate proposals. Instead, they fell back on tradition and their posh lifestyles and lit the revolutionary flame.

THE NATIONAL ASSEMBLY: 1789–1791

EVENTS

June 20, 1789	National Assembly members take Tennis Court Oath, pledging to create new constitution
July 14	Mob of Parisian citizens storms Bastille prison and confiscates weapons
July 20	Rural violence of Great Fear breaks out; peasants lash out at feudal landlords for several weeks
August 4	August Decrees release peasants and farmers from feudal contracts
August 26	Declaration of the Rights of Man and of the Citizen issued
October 5	Parisian women march to Versailles in response to food crisis
February 1790	Government confiscates church property
July 12	Civil Constitution of the Clergy issued

KEY PEOPLE

Louis XVI	French king; was forced to accept August Decrees and Declaration of the Rights of Man and of the Citizen when angry mob of women stormed Versailles in 1789
Jacques Necker	Director general of finance sacked by Louis XVI in 1789; public outrage prompted his reinstatement
Marquis de Lafayette	Nobleman who sided with National Assembly and created French National Guard

THE TENNIS COURT OATH

Three days after splitting from the **Estates-General**, the delegates from the Third Estate (now the **National Assembly**) found themselves locked out of the usual meeting hall and convened on a nearby tennis court instead. There, all but one of the members took the **Tennis Court Oath**, which stated simply that the group would remain indissoluble until it had succeeded in creating a new national constitution.

Upon hearing of the National Assembly's formation, King **Louis XVI** held a general gathering in which the government attempted to intimidate the Third Estate into submission. The assembly, however, had grown too strong, and the king was forced to recognize the group. Parisians had received word of the upheaval, and revolutionary energy coursed through the city. Inspired by the National Assembly, commoners rioted in protest of rising prices. Fearing violence, the king had troops surround his palace at **Versailles**.

THE BASTILLE

Blaming him for the failure of the Estates-General, Louis XVI once again dismissed Director General of Finance **Jacques Necker**.

Necker was a very popular figure, and when word of the dismissal reached the public, hostilities spiked yet again. In light of the rising tension, a scramble for arms broke out, and on July 13, 1789, revolutionaries raided the Paris town hall in pursuit of arms. There they found few weapons but plenty of gunpowder. The next day, upon realizing that it contained a large armory, citizens on the side of the National Assembly stormed the **Bastille**, a medieval fortress and prison in Paris.

Although the weapons were useful, the storming of the Bastille was more symbolic than it was necessary for the revolutionary cause. The revolutionaries faced little immediate threat and had such intimidating numbers that they were capable of nonviolent coercion. By storming one of Paris's most notorious state prisons and hoarding weapons, however, the revolutionaries gained a symbolic victory over the Old Regime and conveyed the message that they were not to be trifled with.

LAFAYETTE AND THE NATIONAL GUARD

As the assembly secured control over the capital, it seemed as if peace might still prevail: the previous governmental council was exiled, and Necker was reinstated. Assembly members assumed top government positions in Paris, and even the king himself traveled to Paris in revolutionary garb to voice his support. To bolster the defense of the assembly, the **Marquis de Lafayette**, a noble, assembled a collection of citizens into the **French National Guard**. Although some blood had already been shed, the Revolution seemed to be subsiding and safely in the hands of the people.

THE GREAT FEAR

For all the developments that were taking place in Paris, the majority of the conflicts erupted in the struggling countryside. Peasants and farmers alike, who had been suffering under high prices and unfair feudal contracts, began to wreak havoc in rural France. After hearing word of the Third Estate's mistreatment by the Estates-General, and feeding off of the infectious revolutionary spirit that permeated France, the peasants amplified their attacks in the countryside over the span of a few weeks, sparking a hysteria dubbed the **Great Fear**. Starting around July 20, 1789, and continuing through the first days of August, the Great Fear spread through sporadic pockets of the French countryside. Peasants attacked country manors and estates, in some cases burning them down in an attempt to escape their feudal obligations.

THE AUGUST DECREES

Though few deaths among the nobility were reported, the **National Assembly**, which was meeting in **Versailles** at the time, feared that the raging rural peasants would destroy all that the assembly had worked hard to attain. In an effort to quell the destruction, the assembly issued the **August Decrees**, which nullified many of the feudal obligations that the peasants had to their landlords. For the time being, the countryside calmed down.

THE DECLARATION OF THE RIGHTS OF MAN AND OF THE CITIZEN

Just three weeks later, on August 26, 1789, the assembly issued the **Declaration of the Rights of Man and of the Citizen**, a document that guaranteed due process in judicial matters and established sovereignty among the French people. Influenced by the thoughts of the era's greatest minds, the themes found in the declaration made one thing resoundingly clear: every person was a Frenchman—and equal. Not surprisingly, the French people embraced the declaration, while the king and many nobles did not. It effectively ended the *ancien régime* and ensured equality for the bourgeoisie. Although subsequent French constitutions that the Revolution produced would be overturned and generally ignored, the themes of the Declaration of Rights of Man and of the Citizen would remain with the French citizenry in perpetuity.

THE FOOD CRISIS

Despite the assembly's gains, little had been done to solve the growing **food crisis** in France. Shouldering the burden of feeding their families, it was the French women who took up arms on October 5, 1789. They first stormed the city hall in Paris, amassing a sizable army and gathering arms. Numbering several thousand, the mob marched to **Versailles**, followed by the National Guard, which accompanied the women to protect them. Overwhelmed by the mob, King **Louis XVI**, effectively forced to take responsibility for the situation, immediately sanctioned the August Decrees and the Declaration of the Rights of Man and of the Citizen. The next day, having little choice, the royal family accompanied the crowd back to Paris. To ensure that he was aware of the woes of the city and its citizens, the king and his family were "imprisoned" in the **Tuileries** Palace in the city

Though they focused on the king as figurehead, most of the revolutionaries were more against the nobles than the king. Everyday people in France had limited interaction with royalty and instead placed blame for the country's problems on the shoulders of local nobility. A common phrase in France at the time was, "If only the king knew," as though he were ignorant of the woes of the people. It was partly owing to this perspective that the assembly attempted to establish a constitutional monarchy alongside the king, rather than simply oust him and rule the nation itself.

THE NATIONAL ASSEMBLY AND THE CHURCH

Over the next two years, the National Assembly took a number of progressive actions to address the failing economy and tighten up the country. A number of them targeted the Catholic Church, which was at the time one of the largest landholders in France. To jump-start the economy, the state in February 1790 confiscated all the church's land and then used it to back a new French currency called the **assignat**. In the beginning, at least, the assignat financed the Revolution and acted as an indicator of the economy's strength.

A short time later, in July 1790, the French Catholic Church itself fell prey to the **Civil Constitution of the Clergy**, a decree by the National Assembly that established a national church system with elected clergy. The country was divided into eighty-three departments, each of which was governed by an elected official and represented by an elected bishop. The voting for these positions was open to anyone who met certain relatively lenient criteria, such as property ownership.

THE ASSEMBLY'S TENUOUS CONTROL

Despite the National Assembly's progress, weaknesses were already being exposed within France, and the Great Fear and the women's march on Versailles demonstrated that perhaps the assembly didn't have as much control as it liked to think. The revolution that the assembly was overseeing in Paris was run almost exclusively by the bourgeoisie, who were far more educated and intelligent than the citizens out in the country. Although the August Decrees helped assuage the peasants' anger, their dissatisfaction would become a recurring problem. The differing priorities that were already apparent foreshadowed future rifts.

Most notable among the assembly's controversial priorities was its treatment of the churches. Although France as a whole was largely secular, large pockets of devoutly religious citizens could be found all over the country. By dissolving the authority of churches, especially the Catholic Church—a move that greatly angered the pope—the assembly seemed to signal to the religious French that they had to make a choice: God or the Revolution. Although this was likely not the case, and certainly not the assembly's intent, it nevertheless upset many people in France.

SUMMARY & ANALYSIS

ESCALATING VIOLENCE: 1791–1792

EVENTS

June 20–21, 1791	Louis XVI and his family flee Paris but are caught near the Austrian border
August 27	Austria and Prussia issue Declaration of Pillnitz
September 14	Louis XVI approves National Assembly's new constitution, which establishes constitutional monarchy
April 20, 1792	France declares war on Austria
August 10	Jacobins and sans-culottes storm Tuileries; depose and arrest Louis XVI
September 2	Sansculottes initiate prison massacres in Paris

KEY PEOPLE

Louis XVI	French king; fled Paris with family in June 1791 but was captured near border with Austria
Jacques-Pierre Brissot	Member of Legislative Assembly and National Convention; driving force behind moderate group called the Girondins
Sansculottes	General term for underrepresented French laborers and commoners who, frustrated that their efforts were largely unrewarded and concerns unrecognized, resorted to mob violence

LOUIS XVI'S FLIGHT

Although King **Louis XVI** maintained a supportive front toward the Revolution, he remained in contact with the rulers of Austria, Prussia, and Sweden, asking for their help in restoring his family to power. In late June 1791, Louis XVI and his family attempted to escape to the Austrian border, where they were supposed to meet the Austrian army and arrange an attack on the revolutionaries. However, the runaway party was caught just before reaching the border and brought back to **Tuileries** in Paris.

This escape attempt considerably weakened the king's position and lowered his regard in the eyes of the French people. Beforehand, although he had little real power remaining, he at least still had the faith of his country. The king's attempt to run away, however, made it clear to skeptics that he was a reluctant associate at best and would turn his back on the constitution and its system of limited monarchy at any moment. The more radical revolutionaries, who had never wanted a constitutional monarchy, trusted the king even less after his attempted escape. The more moderate revolutionaries, who once were staunch proponents of the constitutional monarchy, found themselves hard-pressed to defend a situation in which a monarch was abandoning his responsibilities. Therefore, although

Louis XVI constitutionally retained some power after being returned to Paris, it was clear that his days were numbered.

THE DECLARATION OF PILLNITZ

In response to Louis XVI's capture and forced return to Paris, Prussia and Austria issued the **Declaration of Pillnitz** on August 27, 1791, warning the French against harming the king and demanding that the monarchy be restored. The declaration also implied that Prussia and Austria would intervene militarily in France if any harm came to the king.

Prussia and Austria's initial concern was simply for Louis XVI's well-being, but soon the countries began to worry that the French people's revolutionary sentiment would infect their own citizens. The Declaration of Pillnitz was issued to force the French Revolutionaries to think twice about their actions and, if nothing else, make them aware that other countries were watching the Revolution closely.

THE CONSTITUTION OF 1791

In September 1791, the **National Assembly** released its much-anticipated **Constitution of 1791**, which created a **constitutional monarchy**, or **limited monarchy**, for France. This move allowed King **Louis XVI** to maintain control of the country, even though he and his ministers would have to answer to new legislature, which the new constitution dubbed the **Legislative Assembly**. The constitution also succeeded in eliminating the nobility as a legal order and struck down monopolies and guilds. It established a **poll tax** and barred servants from voting, ensuring that control of the country stayed firmly in the hands of the middle class.

THE JACOBINS AND GIRONDINS

Divisions quickly formed within the new Legislative Assembly, which coalesced into two main camps. On one side were the **Jacobins,** a group of radical liberals—consisting mainly of deputies, leading thinkers, and generally progressive society members—who wanted to drive the Revolution forward aggressively. The Jacobins found Louis's actions contemptible and wanted to forgo the constitutional monarchy and declare France a republic.

Disagreeing with the Jacobins' opinions were many of the more moderate members of the Legislative Assembly, who deemed a constitutional monarchy essential. The most notable of these moderates was **Jacques-Pierre Brissot**. His followers were thus labeled **Brissotins**, although they became more commonly known as **Girondins**.

Many historians have attributed the rivalry of the Jacobins and Girondins to class differences, labeling the Jacobins the poorer, less prestigious of the two groups. However, a number of other factors were involved, as the two groups came from vastly different geographic and ideological backgrounds. The Jacobins were modern urban idealists: they wanted change and independence from any semblance of the *ancien régime*. Deemed radicals, they were students of the enlightened, progressive thought of the time. But the Jacobins, though wanting independence and equality, were more conservative and loyal and harbored less contempt for the monarchy. These fundamental differences would cause a schism that future revolutionary governments in France could not overcome.

The Sansculottes

Meanwhile, in cities throughout France, a group called the sans-culottes began to wield significant and unpredictable influence. The group's name—literally, "without culottes," the knee breeches that the privileged wore—indicated their disdain for the upper classes. The *sans-culottes* consisted mainly of urban laborers, peasants, and other French poor who disdained the nobility and wanted to see an end to privilege. Over the summer of 1792, the *sans-culottes* became increasingly violent and difficult to control.

War Against Austria and Prussia

Although the Girondin leader, Brissot, wanted Louis XVI to remain in power, he felt threatened by the Declaration of Pillnitz and rallied the Legislative Assembly to **declare war** against Austria on April 20, 1792. Austria and Prussia had anticipated this kind of reaction and already had their troops massed along the French border. The French army, unprepared as it was for the battle, was trounced and fled, leaving the country vulnerable to counterattack. In the wake of the embarrassing French defeat, Louis XVI saw to it that Brissot was removed from command. In response, a mob of Girondins marched on Tuileries on June 20 and demanded that Brissot be reinstated. The demand was ignored.

The Storming of Tuileries

Just weeks later, on August 10, anti-monarchy Jacobins rallied together a loyal crew of sans-culottes that stormed Tuileries outright, trashing the palace and capturing Louis XVI and his family as

they tried to escape. The mob then arrested the king for treason. A month after that, beginning on September 2, 1972, the hysterical sans-culottes, having heard rumors of counterrevolutionary talk, raided Paris's prisons and murdered more than 1,000 prisoners.

The Danger of the Sansculottes

If there was any indication throughout the Revolution that no governing body truly had control, it could be found with the sans-culottes. Members of this group were easily swayed and often fell into bouts of mob hysteria, which made them extraordinarily difficult to manage. The bourgeoisie groups "in charge" of the Revolution originally hoped to harness the power of the masses for their own bidding, but it soon became apparent that the sans-culottes were uncontrollable.

The Girondins, who had originally rallied the sans-culottes to their cause, quickly found that the rabble was more radical than they had expected. The massacres that began on September 2 revealed the true power of the sans-culottes and showed the chaos they were capable of creating. The group, after all, consisted of poor workers and peasants who wanted privilege outright eliminated. Despite all their contributions to the revolutionary cause, they still found themselves with little input into the government, which was dominated by bourgeoisie far richer than they. Having gained their freedom from monarchial oppression, the sans-culottes switched their cry from "Liberty!" to "Equality!"

Failures of the Legislative Assembly

Arguably, the Legislative Assembly's complacency in 1792 opened the door to the violence that followed. The assembly did have some cause to rest on its laurels: the Revolution had accomplished everything that had been desired, and the new government had a binder full of legislation to back it up. But the confidence bred by this success was misleading: the assembly had not organized an army that was capable of taking on the combined forces of Austria and Prussia, nor had it sufficiently calmed its own internal feuds. The new government was still far too unsteady even to consider going to war—yet it did, and was soundly defeated. Even more peculiar was the fact that Brissot and his Girondin associates were radical enough to want to go to war, yet conservative enough to do so only under the rule of a constitutional monarch—the same monarch over whom the war was being fought. It was a baffling decision and left little question as to why the Jacobins and other more radical elements wanted to take control.

SUMMARY & ANALYSIS

THE REIGN OF TERROR AND THE THERMIDORIAN REACTION: 1792–1795

EVENTS	
September 22, 1792	France is declared a republic
January 21, 1793	Louis XVI is executed
April 6	National Convention creates Committee of Public Safety
June 24	Constitution of 1793 is established
September 5	Reign of Terror begins; lasts more than ten months
September 29	Robespierre's Maximum implements ceiling on prices
October 16	Marie-Antoinette is executed
July 27, 1794	Robespierre is overthrown
December 24	Maximum is repealed; prices skyrocket

KEY PEOPLE

Louis XVI	French king; executed by new republican government in January 1793
Maximilien Robespierre	Jacobin leader who seized control of National Convention and Committee of Public Safety; later instituted Reign of Terror, targeting those whose philosophies differed from his own
Lazare Carnot	Military strategist who helped reorganize the French war effort and successfully defended the country against foreign invaders
Georges Danton	Longtime Jacobin and close associate of Robespierre who was executed after he began questioning the extremes to which Robespierre was going in the Reign of Terror

THE NATIONAL CONVENTION AND THE FRENCH REPUBLIC

In the autumn of 1792, the revolutionary government, having written off the idea of a constitutional monarchy, set about electing a **National Convention** of delegates to oversee the country. In late September, therefore, the first election took place under the rules of the Constitution of 1791. As it turned out, only a third of the newly elected convention members had sat on a previous assembly, and a great number of new faces belonged to either the **Jacobins** or the **Girondins**. The first action of the convention, on September 21, 1792, was to **abolish the monarchy**. The next day, the **Republic of France** was founded.

THE EXECUTION OF LOUIS XVI

As a sign of the republic's newfound resolve and contempt for the monarchy, the next proposal before the National Convention was the **execution of Louis XVI**. Once again, the moderates objected and eventually forced a trial, but the effort was in vain. Louis XVI was ultimately found guilty of treason and, on January 21, 1793, executed at the guillotine. Months later, on October 16, 1793, his wife, **Marie-Antoinette**, met the same fate.

Symbolically speaking, the declaration of sovereignty and the beheading of the monarch were powerful motivators within France. Unfortunately, the moment of bliss was brief, as the governmental powers quickly realized that all of their achievements were being threatened by internal and external fighting.

THE COMMITTEE OF PUBLIC SAFETY

In the weeks after the execution of the king, the internal and external wars in France continued to grow. Prussian and Austrian forces pushed into the French countryside, and one noted French general even defected to the opposition. Unable to assemble an army out of the disgruntled and protesting peasants, the Girondin-led National Convention started to panic. In an effort to restore peace and order, the convention created the **Committee of Public Safety** on April 6, 1793, to maintain order within France and protect the country from external threats.

THE JACOBINS' COUP

The Committee of Public Safety followed a moderate course after its creation but proved weak and ineffective. After a few fruitless months under the committee, the sans-culottes finally reached their boiling point. They stormed the National Convention and accused the Girondins of representing the aristocracy. Seeing an opportunity, **Maximilien Robespierre**, the leader of the Jacobins, harnessed the fury of the sans-culottes to take control of the convention, banish the Girondins, and install the Jacobins in power.

Once again, the sans-culottes proved to be a formidable force in effecting change during the Revolution. Already upset about the composition of the National Convention—which remained dominated by middle- and upper-class bourgeoisie and was influenced by big thinkers of the time—they became even more angry upon learning that many of the Girondin leaders expected them to bolster the failing war effort. Sieyès had originally rallied the Third Estate by reminding them that they numbered many and that their numbers gave them strength. This message clearly stuck with the sans-culottes throughout the Revolution, and they took advantage of their strength at every possible opportunity.

SUMMARY & ANALYSIS

THE CONSTITUTION OF 1793

Yet another new constitution, the **Constitution of 1793**, premiered in June. However, it was quickly overshadowed by the resurgence of the Committee of Public Safety in July, when some of the more radical Jacobin leaders, including Robespierre, installed themselves in charge of the committee and immediately began to make drastic changes. Among the changes was the suspension of many clauses of the new constitution. One of the most sweeping new Jacobin policies was the **Maximum**, a decree that fixed prices in an attempt to stop the rampant inflation that was ruining the economy.

Although Robespierre soon resorted to extreme measures, his tenure as chairman of the Committee of Public Safety actually began on a productive note. His inspiring, nationalistic propaganda campaign spoke to the disgruntled citizens on their own level. Though he was a lawyer, Robespierre had a middle-class upbringing and could relate to the sans-culottes. His approach to the economy also proved effective in the short run: by using the Maximum to freeze prices, he provided an opportunity for French citizens to get their economic bearings.

CARNOT AND THE MILITARY

In August, military strategist **Lazare Carnot** was appointed head of the French war effort and immediately set about instituting **conscription** throughout France. Propaganda and discipline helped tighten and reenergize the nation, particularly in rural areas. Carnot's effort succeeded, and the newly refreshed army managed to push back the invading Austrian and Prussian forces and reestablish France's traditional boundaries.

THE REIGN OF TERROR

In the autumn of 1793, Robespierre and the Jacobins focused on addressing economic and political threats within France. What began as a proactive approach to reclaiming the nation quickly turned bloody as the government instituted its infamous campaign against internal opposition known as the **Reign of Terror**.

Beginning in September, Robespierre, under the auspices of the Committee of Public Safety, began pointing an accusing finger at anyone whose beliefs seemed to be counterrevolutionary— citizens who had committed no crime but merely had social or political agendas that varied too much from Robespierre's. The committee targeted even those who shared many Jacobin views but were perceived as just slightly too radical or conservative.

A rash of executions ensued in Paris and soon spread to smaller towns and rural areas.

During the nine-month period that followed, anywhere from 15,000 to 50,000 French citizens were beheaded at the **guillotine**. Even longtime associates of Robespierre such as **Georges Danton**, who had helped orchestrate the Jacobin rise to power, fell victim to the paranoia. When Danton wavered in his conviction, questioned Robespierre's increasingly rash actions, and tried to arrange a truce between France and the warring countries, he himself lost his life to the guillotine, in April 1794.

PUBLIC BACKLASH

Robespierre's bloody attempt to protect the sanctity of the Revolution had exactly the opposite result. Rather than galvanize his supporters and the revolutionary nation, the Reign of Terror instead prompted a weakening on every front. Indeed, the Terror accomplished almost nothing productive, as Robespierre quickly burned his bridges and killed many former allies. As the mortuaries started to fill up, the commoners shifted their focus from equality to peace.

By the time the French army had almost completely staved off foreign invaders, Robespierre no longer had a justification for his extreme actions in the name of public "safety." The final straw was his proposal of a "Republic of Virtue," which would entail a move away from the morals of Christianity and into a new set of values. On July 27, 1794, a group of Jacobin allies arrested Robespierre. Receiving the same treatment that he had mandated for his enemies, he lost his head at the guillotine the following day. Undoubtedly, a collective sigh of relief echoed throughout the country.

THE THERMIDORIAN REACTION

With Robespierre out of the picture, a number of the bourgeoisie who had been repressed under the Reign of Terror—many of them Girondins—burst back onto the scene at the **National Convention** in the late summer of 1794. These moderates freed many of the Jacobins' prisoners, neutralized the power of the Committee for Public Safety, and had many of Robespierre's cohorts executed in a movement that became known as the **Thermidorian Reaction**.

However, the moderate and conservative initiatives that the convention subsequently implemented were aimed at the bourgeoisie and undid real accomplishments that Robespierre and his regime had achieved for the poor. To address economic concerns, for instance, the National Convention did away with price controls and printed more money, which allowed prices to sky-rocket. This **inflation** hit the poor hard, and the peasants attempted yet another revolt. However, lacking a strong leader like Robespierre, the peasant uprising was quickly quashed by the government.

THE DIRECTORY: 1795–1799

EVENTS

August 22, 1795	Constitution of 1795 is ratified
October	National Convention is dissolved in favor of five-man executive Directory and two large legislative bodies
May 1796	Coup plot by Gracchus Babeuf and associates is exposed
September 4, 1797	Coup annuls results of legislative elections, removes two directors from power
October 9, 1799	Napoleon returns to France
November 9	Napoleon overthrows the Directory

KEY PEOPLE

Emmanuel-Joseph Sieyès	Theorist and clergy member who maneuvered his way onto the Directory in May 1799 while plotting with Napoleon, enabling Napoleon to take control upon returning to Paris
Napoleon Bonaparte	Young military genius who had great successes in military campaigns in Italy before returning to France in October 1799 and becoming military dictator for fifteen years

SUMMARY & ANALYSIS

THE NEW NATIONAL CONVENTION

The **National Convention** in the era after Robespierre's downfall was significantly more conservative than it had been before and deeply entrenched in the values of the moderate middle class. The change was so drastic that once-powerful groups like the sans-culottes and Jacobins were forced underground, and *sans-culottes* even became a derisive term in France. Meanwhile, the French economy struggled during the winter of 1794–1795, and hunger became widespread.

Although the members of the convention worked diligently to try to establish a new constitution, they faced opposition at every turn. Because many sanctions against the churches had been revoked, the **clergy**—many of whom were still loyal to the royalty—started to return from exile. Likewise, the Comte de Provence, the younger brother of Louis XVI, declared himself next in line for the throne and, taking the name **Louis XVIII**, declared to France that **royalty** would return. (Hopeful French nobles in exile briefly referred to Louis XVI's young son as "Louis XVII," but the boy died in prison in June 1795.)

THE CONSTITUTION OF 1795 AND THE DIRECTORY

On August 22, 1795, the convention was finally able to ratify a new constitution, the **Constitution of 1795**, which ushered in a period of governmental restructuring. The new legislature would consist of two houses: an upper house, called the **Council of Ancients**, consisting of 250 members, and a lower house, called the **Council of Five Hundred**, consisting of 500 members. Fearing influence from the left, the convention decreed that two-thirds of the members of the first new legislature had to have already served on the National Convention between 1792 and 1795.

The new constitution also stipulated that the executive body of the new government would be a group of five officers called the Directory. Although the Directory would have no legislative power, it would have the authority to appoint people to fill the other positions within the government, which was a source of considerable power in itself. **Annual elections** would be held to keep the new government in check.

The dilemma facing the new Directory was a daunting one: essentially, it had to rid the scene of Jacobin influence while at the same time prevent royalists from taking advantage of the disarray and reclaiming the throne. The two-thirds rule was implemented for this reason, as an attempt to keep the same composition like that of the original, moderate-run National Convention. In theory, the new government closely resembled that of the **United States**, with its checks-and-balances system. As it turned out, however, the new government's priorities became its downfall: rather than address the deteriorating economic situation in the country, the legislature instead focused on keeping progressive members out. Ultimately, paranoia and attempts at overprotection weakened the group.

NAPOLEON AND THE FRENCH ARMY

Meanwhile, fortified by the Committee of Public Safety's conscription drive of 1793, the French **army** had grown significantly. While the foundation of the Directory was being laid, the army, having successfully defended France against invasion from Prussia and Austria, kept right on going, blazing its way into foreign countries and annexing land. During the period from 1795 to 1799 in particular, the French army was nearly unstoppable. **Napoleon Bonaparte**, a young Corsican in charge of French forces in Italy and then Egypt, won considerable fame for himself with a series of brilliant victories and also amassed massive reservoirs of wealth and support as he tore through Europe.

The Directory encouraged this French war effort across Europe, though less as a democratic crusade against tyranny than as a means of resolving the unemployment crisis in France. A large, victorious

French army lowered unemployment within France and guaranteed soldiers a steady paycheck to buy the goods they needed to survive. The Directory hoped that this increase in income would encourage an increase in demand, reinvigorating the French economy.

ABUSES BY THE DIRECTORY

Unfortunately, it was not long before the Directory began to abuse its power. The results of the **elections of 1795** were worrisome to the Directory because a number of moderate royalists won. Although these royalists didn't exactly qualify as counterrevolutionaries, their loyalty to the Directory was nevertheless suspect.

Then, in May 1796, a group of Jacobins, led by prominent publisher **Gracchus Babeuf**, met secretly to plan a coup in the hopes of reinstating the government of the Constitution of 1793. Already troubled by the 1795 election results, the Directory squashed the coup plot, had the conspirators arrested, and had Babeuf guillotined.

THE ELECTIONS AND COUP OF 1797

As the **elections of 1797** drew near, the Directory noticed that significant royalist and neo-Jacobin influences were leaking into the republic, which could have terrible implications for the direction of the legislature. On the other hand, the Directory had to obey the Constitution of 1795 and its mandate for annual elections. It therefore allowed the elections to proceed as scheduled.

However, on September 4, 1797, after the elections did indeed produce decidedly pro-royal and pro-Jacobin results, three members of the Directory orchestrated an overthrow of the legislature, **annulling** the election results and removing a majority of the new deputies from their seats. The coup plotters also unseated two members of the Directory itself—former military strategist **Lazare Carnot** being one of them—and installed two new directors, further ensuring that the government would remain staunch in its moderate stance.

POPULAR DISCONTENT

This new Directory was powerfully conservative, initiating strong new financial policies and cracking down on radicalism through executions and other means. However, the coup and the Directory's subsequent abuses of power destroyed all of the government's credibility and further disillusioned the French populace. In the

elections of 1798, the left made gains, feeding on public anger about the coup and the reinstatement of the military **draft.**

The Directory, justifiably fearing the opposition's gains, once again nullified almost one-third of the election results, ensuring that its own policies would remain strongly in place. Public dissatisfaction was an obvious result, and the next elections would have the lowest turnout of any during the Revolution. Meanwhile, **inflation** was continuing unchecked, leading the public to wonder whether a royal return to power wouldn't be more beneficial. Trust and faith in the government neared an all-time low.

FRENCH MILITARY DEFEATS

As the government's credibility took a turn for the worse, so too did French military fortunes. In 1799, Napoleon's seemingly unstoppable forward progress ran into a roadblock in Egypt, and France's army in general faced simultaneous threats from Britain, Austria, Russia, and the Ottoman Empire. Hearing of the bedlam taking place in mainland Europe, as well as within in his own country, Napoleon deserted his men and headed back to France.

SIEYÈS AND THE COUP OF 1799

The failing war efforts amplified the French people's distrust of the Directory, and large majorities of the French public began calling for peace at home and abroad. In May 1799, the upper house of the legislature, the Council of Five Hundred, elected **Emmanuel-Joseph Sieyès**—of "What Is the Third Estate?" fame— to the Directory. This election was the result of extensive maneuvering on Sieyès's part.

Sieyès, however, did not want to keep his newfound power for himself but instead intended to use it to protect the French government from future instability and disturbances. Therefore, he enlisted the aid of Napoleon, with whom he began to plan a **military coup** to topple the very same Directory on which Sieyès himself served. This coup materialized on November 9, 1799, when Napoleon, who had returned to France, overthrew the Directory. The next day, Napoleon dissolved the legislature and instituted himself as first consul, the leader of a **military dictatorship.** By imposing this state of military rule that would grip France for fifteen years, Napoleon effectively ended the French Revolution.

SUMMARY & ANALYSIS

REASONS FOR THE COUP

Although it was the Directory that had encouraged the French army's actions, ultimately, the army's unprecedented success in its outward expansion actually ended up working against the Directory rather than for it. Being away from home for so long, the respective companies of soldiers—particularly those under the control of Napoleon—formed their own identities and group philosophies. By splitting the spoils of each successful campaign with his own troops, Napoleon earned the steadfast devotion of what amounted to a private army. This loyalty would prove essential to the success of his eventual coup and the years of military rule and expansionism that would follow.

Sieyès's political maneuvering may seem inexplicable at first, as he essentially finagled his way into power in the Directory just so he could use that power to remove himself from it. Though that explanation is an oversimplification, it illuminates Sieyès's priorities and demonstrates the depth of the revolutionary spirit that prompted him to make such a sacrifice. To Sieyès, it was clear that, at the time, a military rule under the watch of someone such as Napoleon would be far more beneficial to France than the argumentative, corrupt, and generally ineffective system that was in place. Indeed, though Napoleon would lead as a dictator of sorts, he would do so with much more respect for the spirit of liberty and equality than the originators of the French Revolution had pursued.

Study Questions & Essay Topics

Always use specific historical examples to support your arguments.

Study Questions

1. *Although many accounts of the French Revolution focus on the actions of the Girondins and Jacobins, nearly every major step of the Revolution was incited by the* sans-culottes. *Support or refute this statement.*

A recurring theme throughout the French Revolution was the idea that there is power in numbers, and the sans-culottes represented without doubt the best example of the power of the masses. Although the National Assembly was the governing body during the early stages of the Revolution, it had little control over the symbolic events that incited revolutionary fervor, such as the storming of the Bastille, the Great Fear, and the women's march on Versailles. In fact, it was only in response to these spontaneous, unplanned events that concrete policy changes such as the August Decrees were passed.

Later in the Revolution, the sans-culottes continued to prove influential, as they were involved in the storming of Tuileries, which led to King Louis XVI's deposition, and stormed the National Convention, which gave Robespierre and the Jacobins the opportunity to take control. Although the Reign of Terror and subsequent Thermidorian Reaction suppressed sansculotte activity later in the Revolution, the decline was also due in part to diminished revolutionary spirit and apathy on the part of the government of the Directory. Nevertheless, in the crucial early and middle stages of the Revolution, the sans-culottes proved to be remarkably effective at forcing change—change that otherwise might not have occurred.

2. *Although the financial crisis of the* ancien régime *was the immediate spark that set off the French Revolution, which broader factors within France contributed to the Revolution?*

In adhering to an outdated and essentially baseless feudal system, the aristocracy and monarchy of France provided the true impetus for the French Revolution. In the years leading up to the Revolution, France was riddled with unsustainable economic and cultural disparities: it showed a decadent facade to the world while actually facing catastrophic debt, and boasted some of the greatest minds of the Enlightenment, though its populace was overwhelmingly illiterate and poor.

Perhaps most destabilizing factor was the growing class disparity between the emerging wealthy bourgeoisie and the old nobility. Despite the fact that the nobility were titled and the bourgeoisie were not, many of the bourgeoisie were far wealthier than the "blue-blooded" but financially strapped aristocrats. As the nobility continued to try to claim special privileges over their hardworking bourgeoisie counterparts, it was inevitable that the bourgeoisie would grow angry and resentful.

At the same time, discontent grew among the lower classes as landlords in the countryside continued to bind peasants to outdated, oppressive feudal contracts that were often difficult to fulfill. Simply put, with Enlightenment ideas spreading through France in the late 1700s, it became increasingly obvious that the French nobility wielded a disproportionate amount of power and privilege for no apparent reason. The revolutionaries, with their cries of "Liberty!" and "Equality!", sought to change that.

3. *Assess the validity of this statement: by attempting to escape from France in June 1791, Louis XVI effectively destroyed the prospect of a moderate Revolution resulting in the installation of a limited or constitutional monarchy.*

By definition, a constitutional monarchy needs two things: a constitution and a monarch. By late 1791, France had a constitution, as the National Assembly had presented the new Constitution of 1791 in September. The credibility of the monarch, however, was suspect. Up until his attempted escape from France with his family in June

QUESTIONS & ESSAYS

1791, King Louis XVI had enjoyed vehement backing from moderates within the National Assembly. Jacques-Pierre Brissot and his followers, the Girondins, had sought a constitutional monarchy since the very beginning of the Revolution—much to the chagrin of the radical democratic Jacobins—and had constructed the 1791 constitution around the principle of limited monarchy.

However, the fact that the king tried to run away from the very constitutional monarchy to which he had agreed made it clear that he had given up on the new government. This development made it difficult, if not impossible, for Brissot and the Girondins to defend their pro–constitutional monarchy stance. The Jacobins, who had detested the idea of a king from the beginning, were able to take advantage of the Girondins' weakened position and take control of the government. With Louis XVI having destroyed the credibility of the proposed constitutional monarchy, there was little to prevent the radicals from declaring France a republic, as the Girondins could no longer justify any other feasible form of government.

SUGGESTED ESSAY TOPICS

1. To what extent was the French nobility responsible for the crisis that destroyed the ancien régime?

2. What role did women play in the Revolution? Were they simply a reactionary force—as when bread shortages prompted a march on Versailles—or an active part of the revolutionary public?

3. To what extent did the Thermidorian Reaction owe its success to the excesses of Maximilien Robespierre?

4. Make an argument as to which governmental arrangement—monarchial rule, the National Assembly's constitutional monarchy, the National Convention's republic, or the Directory—was best suited to revolutionary France.

5. What problems in France and beyond contributed to the rise of Napoleon Bonaparte?

Review & Resources

Quiz

1. Which factor did *not* contribute to France's pre-revolution debt?

    A. The Seven Years' War
    B. The cost of maintaining the army and navy
    C. Upkeep at Versailles
    D. High tariffs on imported goods

2. Which was *not* a part of the government at any point during the French Revolution?

    A. The National Convention
    B. The Council of Ancients
    C. The Council of Three Hundred
    D. The Directory

3. What was the name of the French currency that was backed by the value of land acquired from the church?

    A. The argent
    B. The assignat
    C. The franc
    D. The real

4. What type of government did the Constitution of 1791 create?

    A. Limited monarchy
    B. Absolute monarchy
    C. Republic
    D. Communist

5. Who issued the Declaration of Pillnitz?

    A. Baron Manfred von Pillnitz
    B. Great Britain and Norway
    C. Austria and Prussia
    D. Russia and Spain

6. Who created the Committee of Public Safety?

    A. Louis XVI
    B. Maximilien Robespierre
    C. The Directory
    D. The National Convention

7. Which of the following men sat on the original Directory?

    A. Louis XVI
    B. Napoleon
    C. Lazare Carnot
    D. Georges Danton

8. Which of the following men sat on the final Directory?

    A. Napoleon
    B. Emmanuel-Joseph Sieyès
    C. Honoré de Balzac
    D. Jacques-Pierre Brissot

9. Who shot down Charles de Calonne's debt-relief-by-taxation proposal?

    A. The Assembly of Notables
    B. Louis XVI
    C. The National Assembly
    D. The Estates-General

10. Before 1789, when was the Estates-General last assembled?

    A. 1492
    B. 1614
    C. 1756
    D. 1066

11. According to Emmanuel-Joseph Sieyès's pamphlet, what is the Third Estate?

    A.   Versailles
    B.   The Nation
    C.   The royalty
    D.   A rip-off

12. What did the Tennis Court Oath establish?

    A.   That no one would be Louis XVI's doubles partner
    B.   That the Third Estate would accept the tax burden in return for freedom from feudal contracts
    C.   That the National Assembly wouldn't dissolve until they had created a constitution
    D.   That France would no longer support the Catholic Church

13. Who helped form the French National Guard?

    A.   Maximilien Robespierre
    B.   Lazare Carnot
    C.   Napoleon
    D.   Marquis de Lafayette

14. Which Parisian landmark was raided by revolutionaries in pursuit of arms?

    A.   The Bastille
    B.   The Louvre
    C.   The Musée d'Orsay
    D.   Versailles

15. Which period was known as the Great Fear?

    A. 1786–1789, when it was clear that France's economic situation was dire

    B. The summer of 1789, when peasants around the French countryside revolted against their feudal landlords

    C. 1793–1794, when Robespierre systematically killed more than 15,000 alleged counter revolutionary activists

    D. 1797–1799, when the corrupt Directory ruled dictatorially

16. What problem did the August Decrees eliminate?

    A. The bread shortage

    B. The oppressive feudal contracts to which peasants were bound

    C. Uncontrolled inflation

    D. Syphilis

17. What happened on August 26, 1789?

    A. Marie-Antoinette was executed

    B. The Estates-General convened

    C. The Declaration of the Rights of Man and of the Citizen was issued

    D. Georges Danton and Maximilien Robespierre played tennis

18. Which event did not take place during the summer of 1789?

    A. The Tennis Court Oath

    B. The Great Fear

    C. The Reign of Terror

    D. The August Decrees

REVIEW & RESOURCES

19. Which of the following was *not* an element of monarchial rule in France?

    A. Divine right
    B. Absolute rule
    C. Birthright
    D. Electoral accountability

20. What did the Second Estate comprise?

    A. The clergy
    B. The bourgeoisie
    C. The peasantry
    D. The nobility

21. When was the Tennis Court Oath taken?

    A. June 20, 1789
    B. July 20, 1789
    C. August 20, 1789
    D. July 20, 1791

22. What was the main reason that several thousand women marched on Versailles in October 1789?

    A. Bread shortages in Paris
    B. Universal suffrage for men and women
    C. An influenza outbreak
    D. An exhibition of Marie-Antoinette's fashions

23. France celebrates July 14 as a holiday because it is the anniversary of

    A. The storming of the Bastille
    B. The Tennis Court Oath
    C. The beginning of the First French Republic
    D. The death of Robespierre

24. Marie-Antoinette was the wife of which French monarch?

    A. Napoleon
    B. Louis XIV
    C. Louis XV
    D. Louis XVI

REVIEW & RESOURCES

25. Which of the following rallying cries best describes the second stage of the French Revolution?

    A.   "God and the king!"
    B.   "Equality!"
    C.   "Liberty!"
    D.   "Bread and peace!"

26. Which of the following lists of events is in correct chronological order (from earliest to latest)?

    A.   Estates-General convenes; Civil Constitution of the Clergy is issued; Louis XVI is executed; storming of the Bastille
    B.   National Assembly is established; Reign of Terror; Declaration of Pillnitz; Louis XVI attempts to flee France
    C.   Tennis Court Oath; storming of the Bastille; First Republic is declared; Reign of Terror
    D.   The Directory takes dictatorial powers; Napoleon overthrows the Directory; Robespierre is executed, Declaration of Pillnitz

27. Which of the following did *not* occur?

    A.   Robespierre eliminated all economic controls and allowed prices to rise sharply
    B.   Louis XVI attempted to flee France
    C.   The Jacobins took control of the National Convention away from the Girondins
    D.   For a time, the French government was a limited monarchy

28. Which party wanted a limited monarchy in France?

    A.   Moderates
    B.   Monarchists
    C.   Jacobins
    D.   None of the above

29. Who issued the Civil Constitution of the Clergy?

   A. The National Convention
   B. Louis XVI
   C. The Committee of Public Safety
   D. The National Assembly

30. Which of the following would *not* have been grouped under the Third Estate?

   A. Priests
   B. Merchants
   C. The bourgeoisie
   D. Peasants

31. Which of the following is probably *not* a reason why the French Revolution turned violent?

   A. Severe food shortages
   B. The fact that the peasantry was in control
   C. The heavy tax burden on the poor
   D. The threat of foreign attack

32. When did the people of Paris storm the Tuileries Palace?

   A. October 5, 1790
   B. June 17, 1789
   C. August 10, 1792
   D. September 22, 1792

33. Which document effectively nationalized the French church?

   A. The Declaration of the Rights of Man and of the Citizen
   B. The Constitution of 1791
   C. The Civil Constitution of the Clergy
   D. The Concordat of Worms

REVIEW & RESOURCES

34. Which document created a limited monarchy?

   A. The Declaration of the Rights of Man and of the Citizen
   B. The Constitution of 1791
   C. The Civil Constitution of the Clergy
   D. The Concordat of Worms

35. Which document declared that all men are free and equal?

   A. The Declaration of the Rights of Man and of the Citizen
   B. The Constitution of 1791
   C. The Civil Constitution of the Clergy
   D. The Concordat of Worms

36. Why do some historians consider the passage of the Civil Constitution of the Clergy to be a mistake?

   A. It increased the size of the clergy and reduced the number of available soldiers
   B. It empowered the conservative institution of the church against the Revolution
   C. It turned France into a Protestant state
   D. It created a dilemma for the devout masses of France, forcing them to choose between the Revolution and God

37. Which group was most likely in favor of a limited monarchy?

   A. The Jacobins
   B. The monarchists
   C. The Girondins
   D. The aristocracy

38. Which group was most likely in favor of the principle of privilege and feudal obligations?

   A. The Jacobins
   B. The monarchists
   C. The Girondins
   D. The aristocracy

39. Which group was most likely in favor of absolute rule by dynasty?

    A. The Jacobins
    B. The monarchists
    C. The Girondins
    D. The aristocracy

40. Which group was most likely in favor of the system of one vote per estate in the Estates-General?

    A. The Jacobins
    B. The monarchists
    C. The Girondins
    D. The aristocracy

41. Which of the following lists of events is in correct chronological order (from earliest to latest)?

    A. Parisian women march on Versailles; storming of the Tuileries; Reign of Terror; First Republic
    B. Storming of the Tuileries; Reign of Terror, Parisian Women march on Versailles; First Republic
    C. Storming of the Tuileries; Parisian women march on Versailles; First Republic; Reign of Terror
    D. Parisian women march on Versailles; storming of the Tuileries; First Republic; Reign of Terror

42. In which position did Napoleon begin his career?

    A. Government bureaucrat
    B. Army officer
    C. Doctor
    D. Landlord

43. How were the French aristocracy taxed during the time of Louis XVI?

    A. They were not taxed
    B. They were taxed in proportion to landholdings
    C. They were taxed in proportion to total net worth
    D. They paid primarily sales taxes

44. To which country were Louis XVI and his family trying to escape when they were captured?

   A. Austria
   B. Spain
   C. Britain
   D. Germany

45. Why did the radical group of commoners call themselves sans-culottes?

   A. They refused to wear pants
   B. They were distinguishing themselves from the upper class, with its high fashion
   C. The army had commandeered their culottes
   D. None of the above

46. When did the National Assembly confiscate church property?

   A. June 1790
   B. May 1789
   C. February 1790
   D. April 1792

47. Which of the following was *not* a revolutionary figure?

   A. Maximilien Robespierre
   B. Francis II Habsburg
   C. Marquis de Lafayette
   D. Jacques Pierre Brissot

48. For how many years did Napoleon Bonaparte rule France after overthrowing the Directory?

   A. Fifteen
   B. Twenty
   C. Twenty-five
   D. Thirty

49. What took place following the 1797 election?

   A. The royal family regained control of France
   B. Napoleon was elected first consul
   C. Pregnant chads stirred up controversy
   D. The government was unhappy with the results and
      annulled a majority of them

50. Which early Girondin leader pushed for war following the
    Declaration of Pillnitz and was later executed when the
    Jacobins took control?

   A. Marquis de Lafayette
   B. Maximilien Robespierre
   C. Charles de Calonne
   D. Jacques-Pierre Brissot

SUGGESTIONS FOR FURTHER READING

CHARTIER, ROGER. *The Cultural Origins of the French Revolution.*
Durham, North Carolina: Duke University Press, 1991.

COBB, RICHARD. *The French and Their Revolution.* New York:
New Press, 1998.

EGENDORF, LAURA K, ED. *The French Revolution: Opposing
Viewpoints in World History.* Farmington Hills, Michigan:
Greenhaven Press, 2004.

FURET, FRANCOIS. *Interpreting the French Revolution.* New York:
Cambridge University Press, 1981.

GERSHOY, LEO. *The Era of the French Revolution, 1789–1799.*
New York: Van Nostrand, 1957.

HIGONNET, PATRICE. *Class, Ideology, and the Rights of Nobles
During the French Revolution.* Cambridge, Massachusetts:
Harvard University Press, 1981.

LEFEBVRE, GEORGES. *The Coming of the French Revolution.* New
York: Vintage Books, 1947.

PALMER, R. R. *The Age of Democratic Revolution.* Princeton, New
Jersey: Princeton University Press, 1959.

ROBERTS, J. M. *The French Revolution.* New York: Oxford
University Press, 1997.

RUDE, GEORGE. *The French Revolution.* New York: Grove Press,
1988.

SUTHERLAND, D. M. G. *France 1789–1815: Revolution and
Counterrevolution.* New York: Oxford University Press, 1986.

VOVELLE, MICHEL. *The Fall of the French Monarchy 1787–1792.*
New York: Cambridge University Press, 1984.

REVIEW & RESOURCES